# My Sight Word List

English - Portuguese

| | | |
|---|---|---|
| a | in | said |
| and | is | see |
| away | it | the |
| big | jump | three |
| blue | little | to |
| can | look | two |
| come | make | up |
| down | me | we |
| find | my | where |
| for | not | yellow |
| funny | one | you |
| go | day | |
| help | play | |
| here | red | |
| I | run | |

Name: __________________  Date: __________________

Today is:  Monday   Tuesday   Wednesday
           Thursday   Friday

Direction: Trace and read the sentences.

| bag | rag | tag | wag |
|---|---|---|---|
| saco | trapo | tag | abanando |

He has many bags.

I see a rag.

I see a tag.

Its tail is wagging.

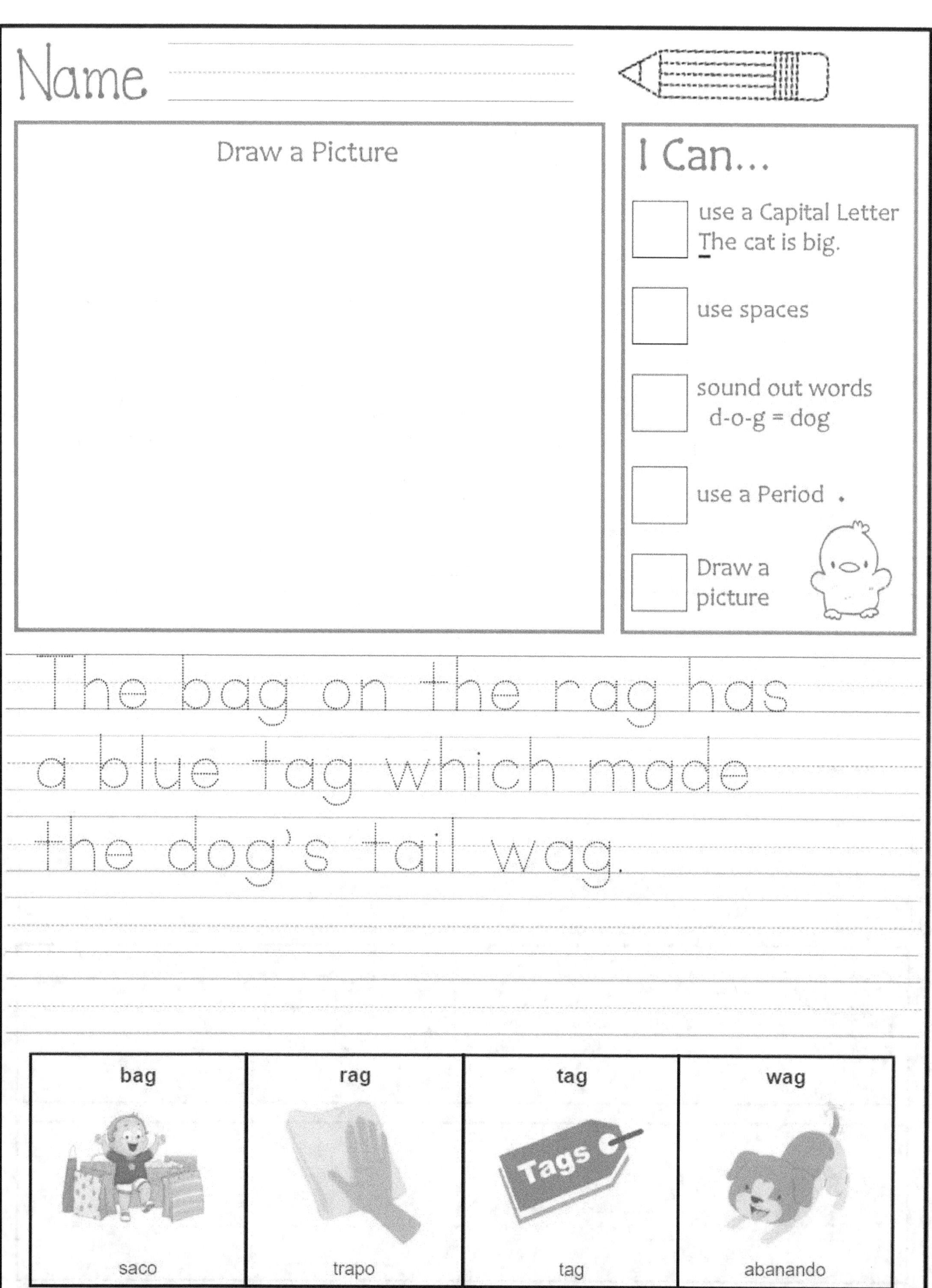


Name

Draw a Picture

I Can...

use a Capital Letter
The cat is big.

use spaces

sound out words
d-o-g = dog

use a Period .

Draw a
picture

The bag on the rag has
a blue tag which made
the dog's tail wag.

bag
saco

rag
trapo

tag
tag

wag
abanando

Name: _________________________  Date: _______________

Today is: [ Monday ] [ Tuesday ] [ Wednesday ]
[ Thursday ] [ Friday ]

Direction: Trace and read the sentences.

| **can** | **man** | **pan** | **van** |
|---|---|---|---|
| latas | cara | panela | furgão |

I see a can of soda.

The man is happy.

The pan is dirty.

I see a big van.

The man who was driving a van ran over a can and a pan.

| can | man | pan | van |
|---|---|---|---|
| latas | cara | panela | furgão |

Name: _________________________ Date: _________________

Today is: [Monday] [Tuesday] [Wednesday]
[Thursday] [Friday]

Direction: Trace and read the sentences.

| **cut** | **gut** | **hut** | **nut** |
| --- | --- | --- | --- |
| cortar | intestino | cabana | noz |

He cut his nails.

He has a gut.

This is a small hut.

It is holding a nut.

Name ____________________

### Draw a Picture

## I Can...

- [ ] use a Capital Letter
  The cat is big.

- [ ] use spaces

- [ ] sound out words
  d-o-g = dog

- [ ] use a Period .

- [ ] Draw a picture

A boy swallowed a nut and it got stuck in his belly. He had to get his gut cut open in the hut.

| cut | gut | hut | nut |
|-----|-----|-----|-----|
| cortar | intestino | cabana | noz |

Name: _______________ Date: _______________

Today is: Monday | Tuesday | Wednesday | Thursday | Friday

Direction: Trace and read the sentences.

| fat | cat | hat | mat |
| --- | --- | --- | --- |
| gordura | gato | chapéu | esteira |

I see a fat dog.

This is my little cat.

I like this hat.

I see a big mat.

Draw a Picture

## I Can...

- ☐ use a Capital Letter
  The cat is big.

- ☐ use spaces

- ☐ sound out words
  d-o-g = dog

- ☐ use a Period .

- ☐ Draw a picture

The fat cat laid on the mat that was a hat pattern.

| fat | cat | hat | mat |
|-----|-----|-----|-----|
| gordura | gato | chapéu | esteira |

Name: _______________  Date: _______________

Today is: [ Monday ] [ Tuesday ] [ Wednesday ]
[ Thursday ] [ Friday ]

Direction: Trace and read the sentences.

| cab | lab | tab | crab |
|-----|-----|-----|------|
| táxi | laboratório | aba | caranguejo |

The cab is fast.

The lab is exciting.

The tab is long.

We found a crab.

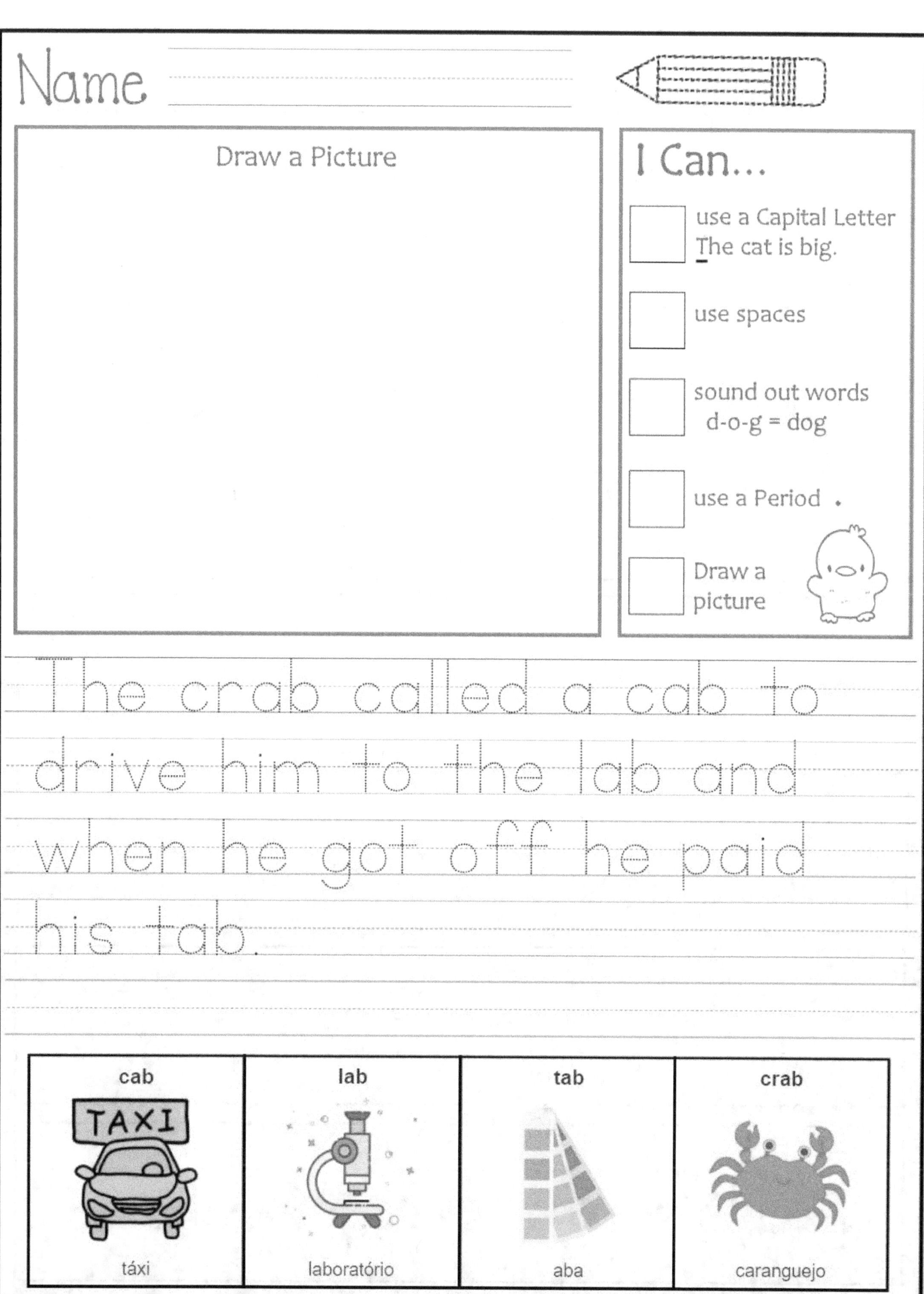

Name

Draw a Picture

I Can...

use a Capital Letter
The cat is big.

use spaces

sound out words
d-o-g = dog

use a Period .

Draw a
picture

The crab called a cab to
drive him to the lab and
when he got off he paid
his tab.

cab
táxi

lab
laboratório

tab
aba

crab
caranguejo

Name: ____________________ Date: ____________________

Today is: Monday | Tuesday | Wednesday | Thursday | Friday

Direction: Trace and read the sentences.

| ham | jam | ram | clam |
| --- | --- | --- | --- |
|  |  |  |  |
| presunto | geléia | ovelha | concha |

I like to eat ham.

We like to eat jam.

The ram is big.

The clam is pretty.

# Name

Draw a Picture

## I Can...

- [ ] use a Capital Letter
  The cat is big.

- [ ] use spaces

- [ ] sound out words
  d-o-g = dog

- [ ] use a Period .

- [ ] Draw a picture

The clam gave the ram ham. Then the ram gave the clam jam.

| ham | jam | ram | clam |
|---|---|---|---|
| presunto | geléia | ovelha | concha |

| bed | led | red | wed |
|---|---|---|---|
| cama | conduzindo | vermelho | casamento |

This is my little bed.

He led us to safety.

The apple is red.

He asks her to wed.

Name ____________________________

<table>
<tr><td>Draw a Picture</td><td>## I Can...</td></tr>
</table>

## I Can...

- [ ] use a Capital Letter
  <u>T</u>he cat is big.

- [ ] use spaces

- [ ] sound out words
  d-o-g = dog

- [ ] use a Period .

- [ ] Draw a picture

When the prince got out of bed, he was led on a red carpet to be wed with the princess.

| bed | led | red | wed |
|-----|-----|-----|-----|
| cama | conduzindo | vermelho | casamento |

Name: _______________ Date: _______________

Today is: [ Monday ] [ Tuesday ] [ Wednesday ]
[ Thursday ] [ Friday ]

Direction: Trace and read the sentences.

| bad | dad | mad | sad |
|---|---|---|---|
| ruim | papai | louco | triste |

This apple is bad.

My dad is very kind.

The reindeer is mad.

The little cat is sad.

I was bad so my dad
got mad and now
I am so sad.

| bad | dad | mad | sad |
|---|---|---|---|
| ruim | papai | louco | triste |

Name: ______________________ Date: ______________________

Today is: Monday Tuesday Wednesday Thursday Friday

Direction: Trace and read the sentences.

| den | hen | pen | ten |
|---|---|---|---|
|  |  |  | 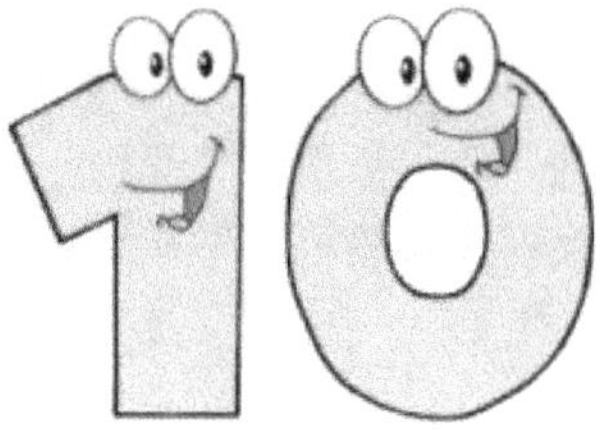 |
| covil | galinha | estábulos | dez |

It is a den.

The hens lay eggs.

She has a good pen.

The ten is smiling.

## Draw a Picture

### I Can...

- [ ] use a Capital Letter
  <u>T</u>he cat is big.

- [ ] use spaces

- [ ] sound out words
  d-o-g = dog

- [ ] use a Period .

- [ ] Draw a picture

The hen that lived in the
pen laid ten eggs
in her den.

| den | hen | pen | ten |
|-----|-----|-----|-----|
| covil | galinha | estábulos | dez |

Name: ____________________ Date: ____________________

Today is: Monday | Tuesday | Wednesday | Thursday | Friday

Direction: Trace and read the sentences.

| gum | mum | sum | drum |
|---|---|---|---|
|  |  |  |  |
| gomoso | mãe | soma | tambor |

I like to chew gum.

My mum is kind!

I can do a sum!

The drum is big.

Draw a Picture

## I Can...

- [ ] use a Capital Letter
  The cat is big.
- [ ] use spaces
- [ ] sound out words
  d-o-g = dog
- [ ] use a Period .
- [ ] Draw a picture

Mum was chewing gum while figuring out the sum of the drum's price.

| **gum** | **mum** | **sum** | **drum** |
|---|---|---|---|
| gomoso | mãe | soma | tambor |

Name: _________________________ Date: _______________

Today is: Monday  Tuesday  Wednesday

Thursday  Friday

Direction: Trace and read the sentences.

| **bid** | **hid** | **kid** | **lid** |
|---|---|---|---|
| licitação | ocultar | criança | tampa |

He likes to bid.

He is hiding.

The kid like to play.

I see a lid.

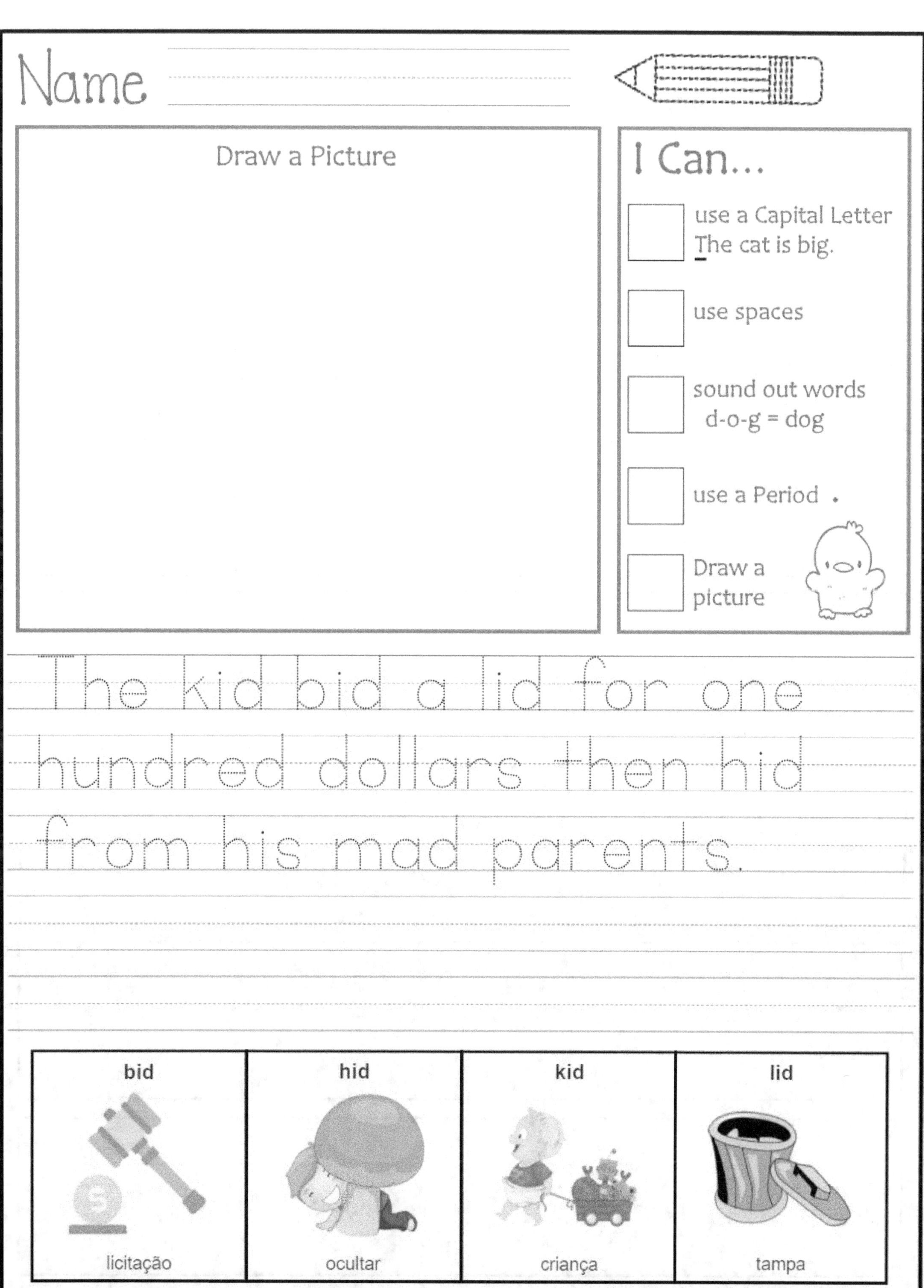


Name

Draw a Picture

I Can...

use a Capital Letter
The cat is big.

use spaces

sound out words
d-o-g = dog

use a Period .

Draw a
picture

The kid bid a lid for one
hundred dollars then hid
from his mad parents.

bid

hid

kid

lid

licitação

ocultar

criança

tampa

Name: _________________________ Date: _______________

Today is: [ Monday ] [ Tuesday ] [ Wednesday ]
[ Thursday ] [ Friday ]

Direction: Trace and read the sentences.

| **big** | **dig** | **pig** | **wig** |
| grande | escavação | porco | peruca |

That is a big pencil.

He will dig up a hole.

The pig is fat.

She puts on a wig.

Name

Draw a Picture

## I Can...

- [ ] use a Capital Letter
  The cat is big.
- [ ] use spaces
- [ ] sound out words
  d-o-g = dog
- [ ] use a Period .
- [ ] Draw a picture

The big pig went to dig
in the mud for his wig.

| **big** | **dig** | **pig** | **wig** |
|---|---|---|---|
|  |  |  |  |
| grande | escavação | porco | peruca |

Name: _________________________  Date: _______________

Today is: [Monday] [Tuesday] [Wednesday]
[Thursday] [Friday]

Direction: Trace and read the sentences.

| **bin** | **fin** | **pin** | **win** |
| --- | --- | --- | --- |
| bin | barbatana | pin | ganhar |

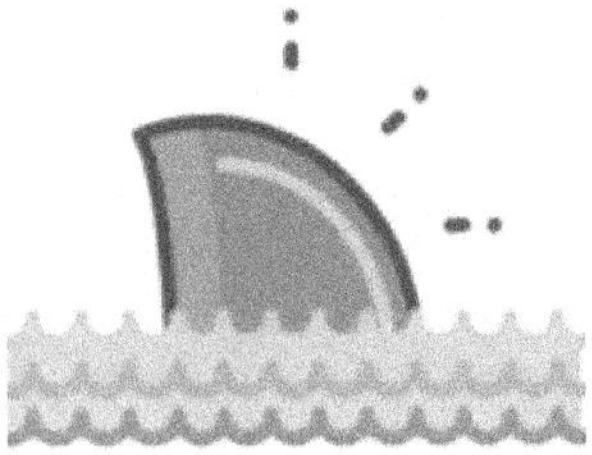

It is a recycle bin.

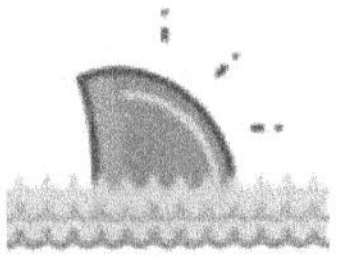

The shark has a fin.

The pin is pointy.

He won the match.

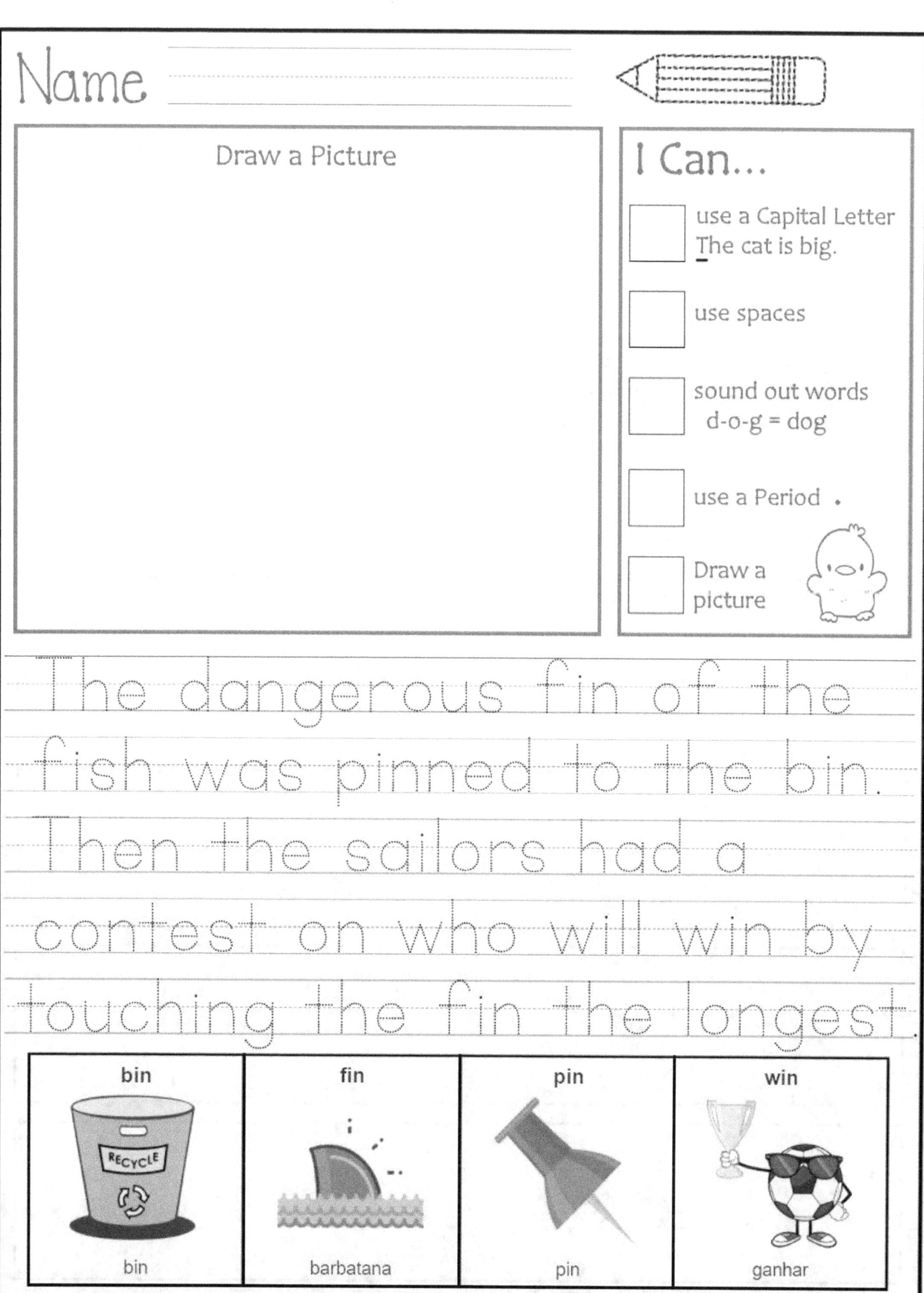

Name

Draw a Picture

## I Can...

- [ ] use a Capital Letter
  The cat is big.
- [ ] use spaces
- [ ] sound out words
  d-o-g = dog
- [ ] use a Period .
- [ ] Draw a picture

The dangerous fin of the fish was pinned to the bin. Then the sailors had a contest on who will win by touching the fin the longest.

| bin | fin | pin | win |
|-----|-----|-----|-----|
| bin | barbatana | pin | ganhar |

Name: _________________________ Date: _________________________

Today is: [ Monday ] [ Tuesday ] [ Wednesday ]
[ Thursday ] [ Friday ]

Direction: Trace and read the sentences.

| hip | lip | nip | sip |
|---|---|---|---|
| quadril | lábios | beliscar | bebida |

This is my hip.

Her lips are red.

It is nipping its toy.

She is sipping.

Draw a Picture

I Can...

☐ use a Capital Letter
The cat is big.

☐ use spaces

☐ sound out words
d-o-g = dog

☐ use a Period .

☐ Draw a picture

The dog nipped someone who was sipping water with his lip.

| hip | lip | nip | sip |
|-----|-----|-----|-----|
| quadril | lábios | beliscar | bebida |

Name: _________________ Date: _________________

Today is: [ Monday ] [ Tuesday ] [ Wednesday ]
[ Thursday ] [ Friday ]

Direction: Trace and read the sentences.

| **fit** | **hit** | **kit** | **sit** |
|---|---|---|---|
| em forma | acertar | kit | sentar |

It is perfectly fit.

They hit each other.

That is a safety kit.

He is sitting.

Draw a Picture

## I Can...

- [ ] use a Capital Letter
  The cat is big.
- [ ] use spaces
- [ ] sound out words
  d-o-g = dog
- [ ] use a Period .
- [ ] Draw a picture

The fit doctor sat then was hit by a kit.

| fit | hit | kit | sit |
|---|---|---|---|
| em forma | acertar | kit | sentar |

Name: _________________ Date: _______________

Today is: Monday  Tuesday  Wednesday  Thursday  Friday

Direction: Trace and read the sentences.

| cob | job | rob | sob |
| --- | --- | --- | --- |
| milho | trabalho | roubar | chorar |

I ate corn on the cob

This is my job.

He is robbing.

The girl is sobbing.

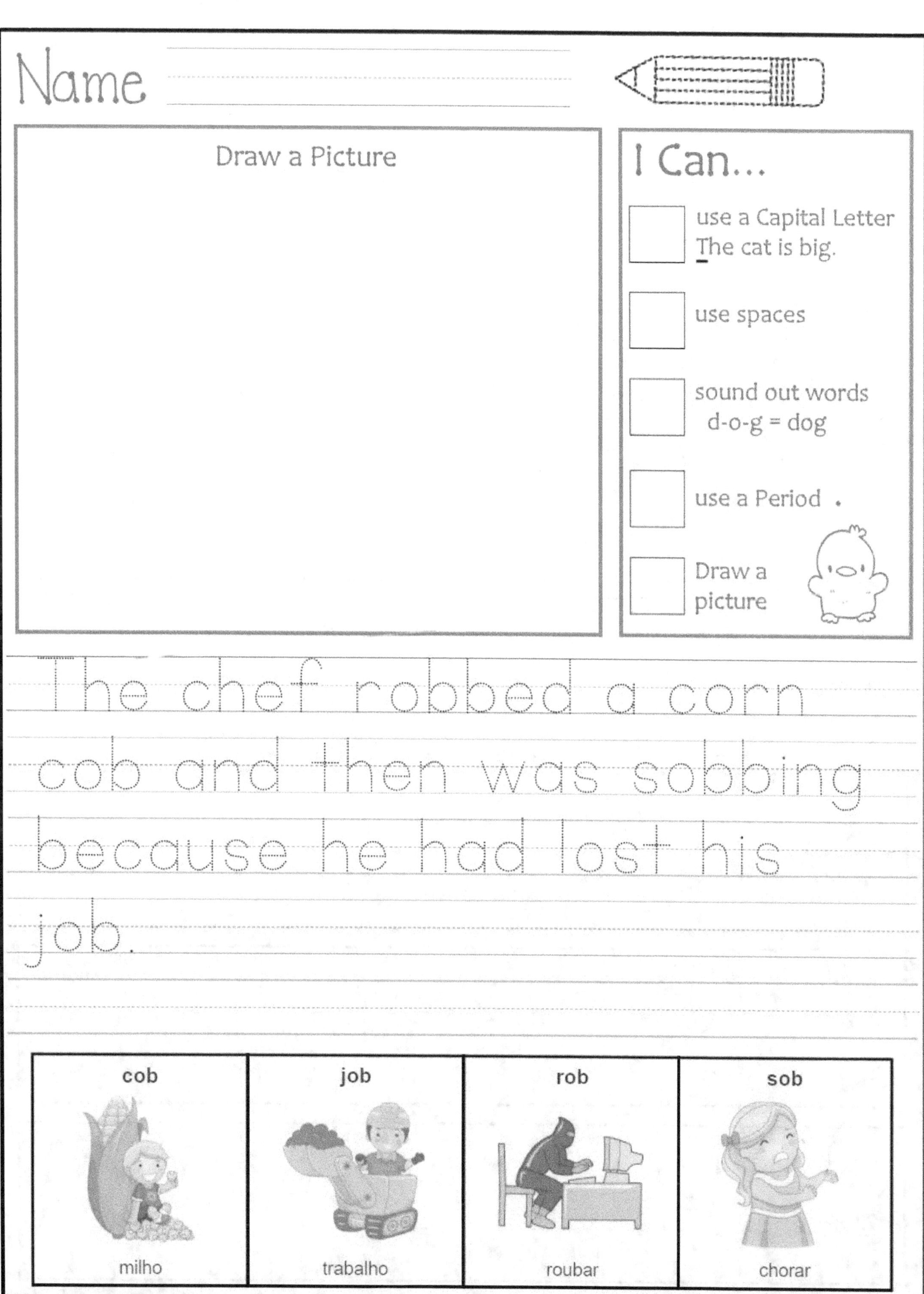


Name

Draw a Picture

I Can...

use a Capital Letter
The cat is big.

use spaces

sound out words
d-o-g = dog

use a Period .

Draw a
picture

The chef robbed a corn
cob and then was sobbing
because he had lost his
job.

cob

milho

job

trabalho

rob

roubar

sob

chorar

Name: ______________________ Date: ______________________

Today is: Monday Tuesday Wednesday Thursday Friday

Direction: Trace and read the sentences.

| dog | hog | jog | log |
| --- | --- | --- | --- |
|  |  |  | 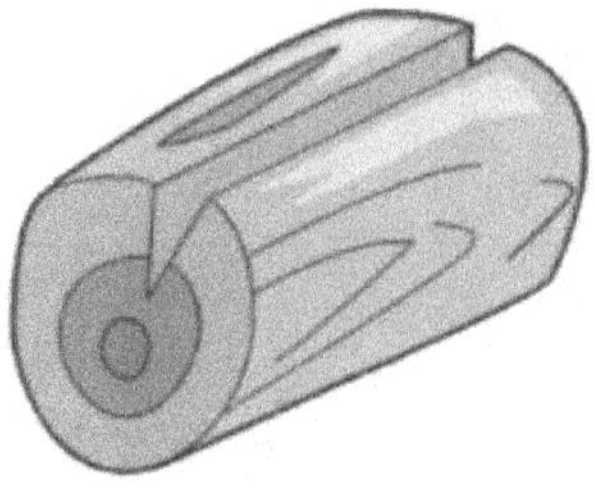 |
| cão | porco | corrida | madeira |

The dog is thrilled.

The hog is big.

She is jogging.

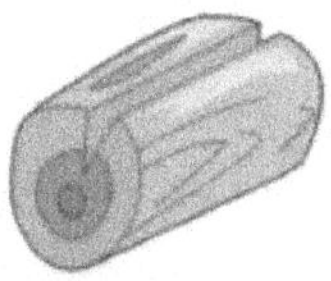

The log is small.

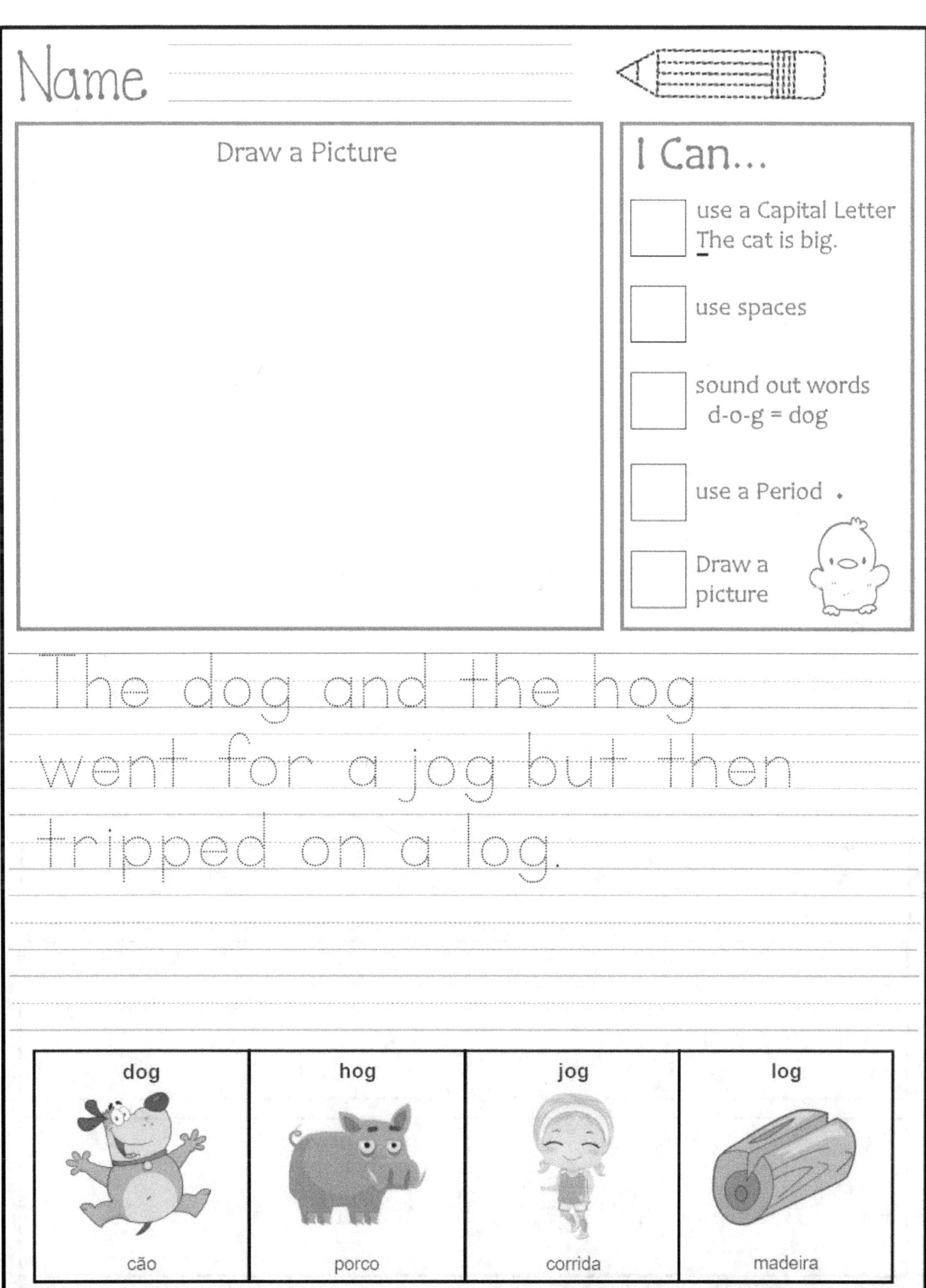

Name

Draw a Picture

I Can...

use a Capital Letter
The cat is big.

use spaces

sound out words
d-o-g = dog

use a Period .

Draw a
picture

The dog and the hog
went for a jog but then
tripped on a log.

dog
cão

hog
porco

jog
corrida

log
madeira

Name: ____________________ Date: ____________________

Today is: Monday | Tuesday | Wednesday | Thursday | Friday

Direction: Trace and read the sentences.

| bug | hug | jug | mug |
| --- | --- | --- | --- |
| 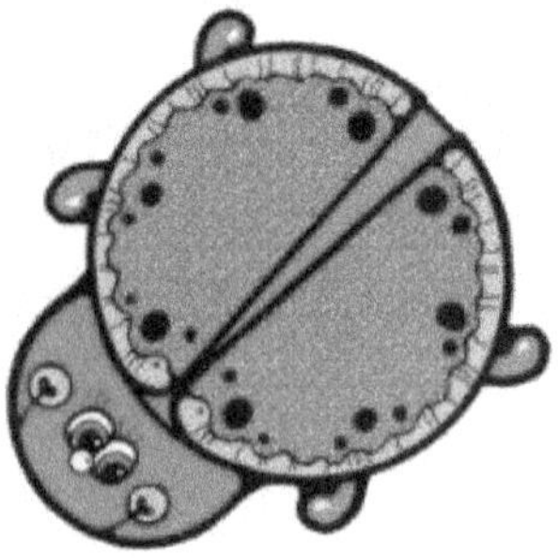 |  |  |  |
| erro | abraço | jarro | caneca |

 The bug is colorful.

 She is hugging.

 The jug has milk in it.

 He has a mug.

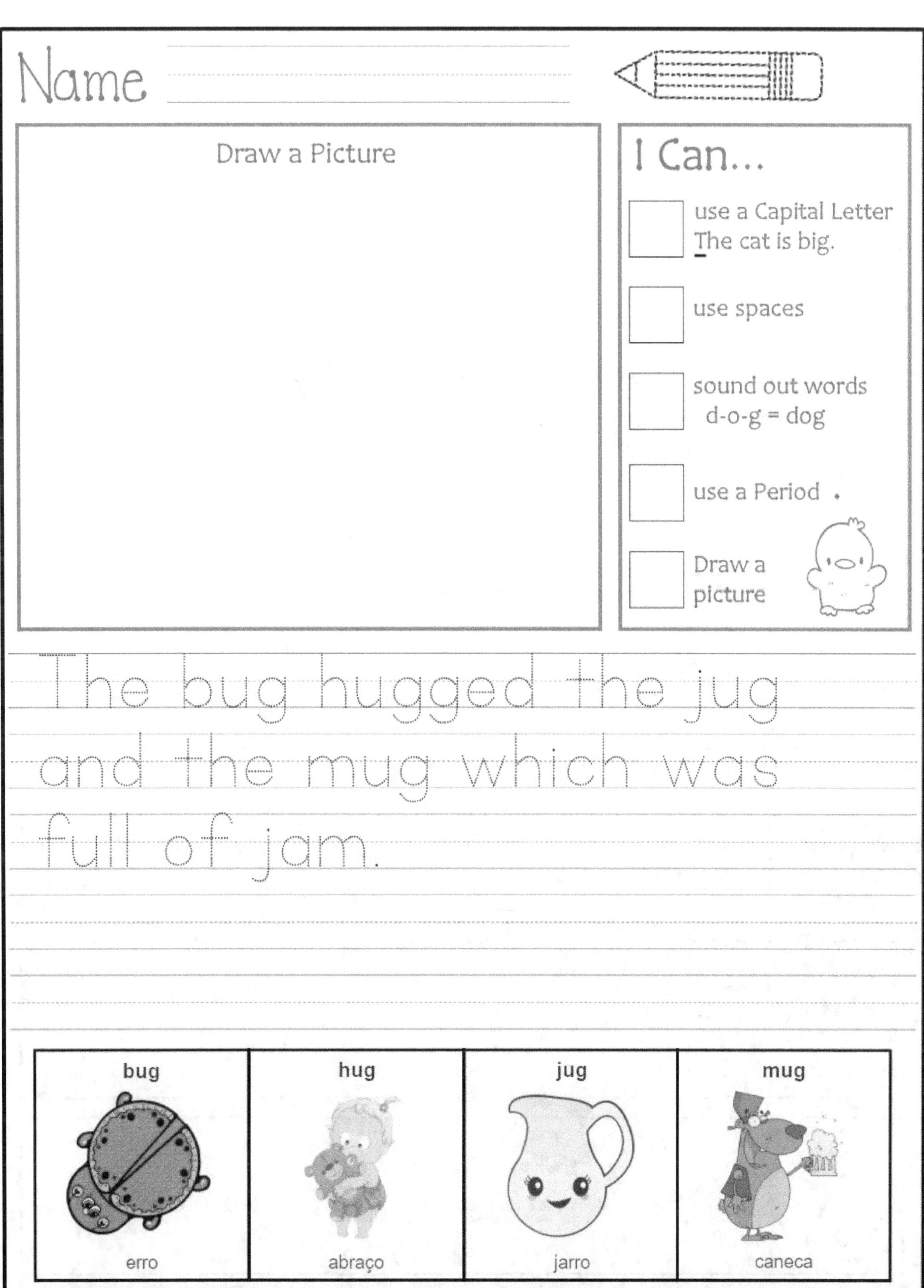

Name

Draw a Picture

## I Can...

- [ ] use a Capital Letter
  The cat is big.
- [ ] use spaces
- [ ] sound out words
  d-o-g = dog
- [ ] use a Period .
- [ ] Draw a picture

The bug hugged the jug
and the mug which was
full of jam.

| bug | hug | jug | mug |
| --- | --- | --- | --- |
| erro | abraço | jarro | caneca |

Name: __________________ Date: __________________

Today is: [Monday] [Tuesday] [Wednesday]
[Thursday] [Friday]

Direction: Trace and read the sentences.

| cot | dot | hot | pot |
|---|---|---|---|
| cama | ponto | quente | panela |

This is my cot.

There are many dots.

It is very hot.

He has a plant pot.

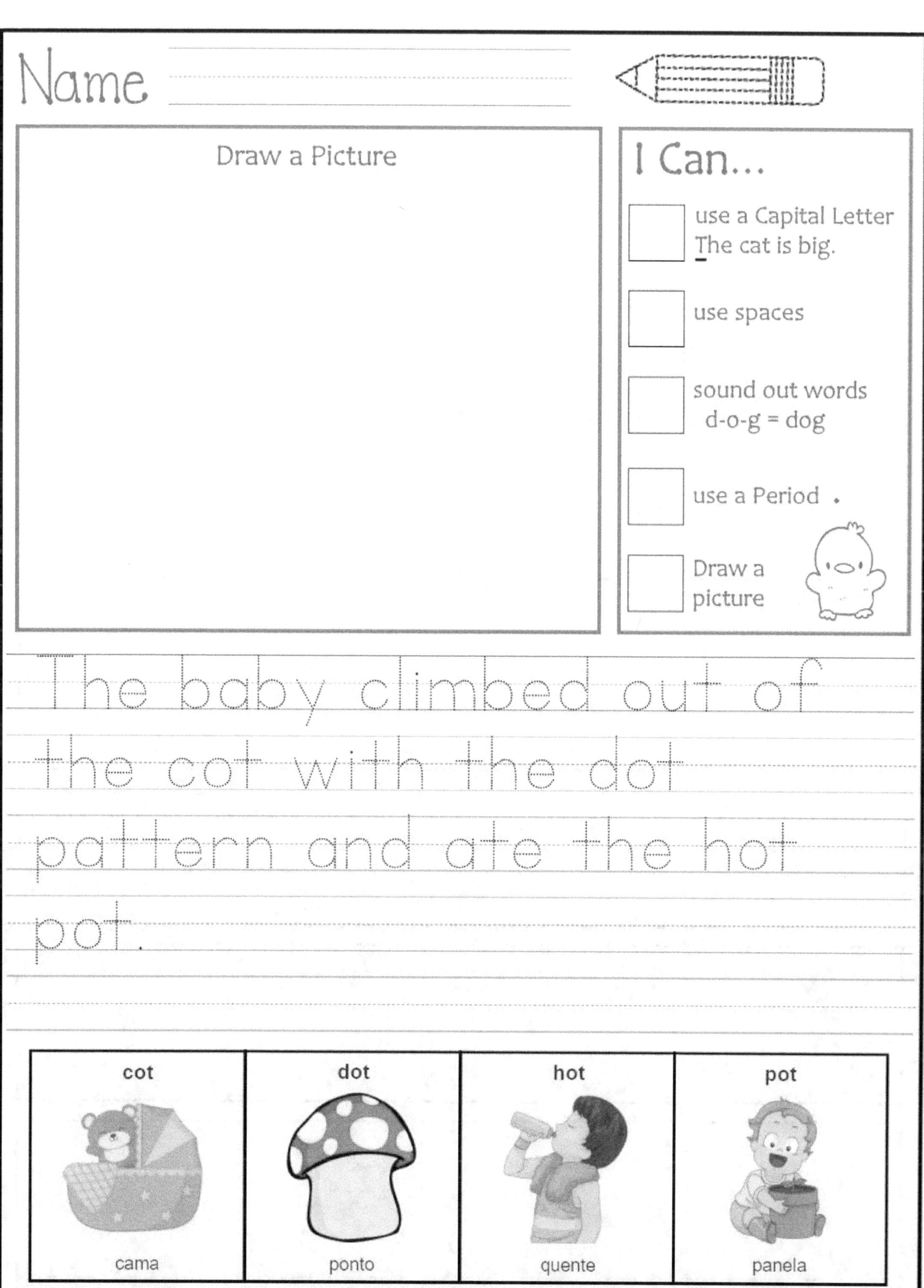

Name

Draw a Picture

I Can...

use a Capital Letter
The cat is big.

use spaces

sound out words
d-o-g = dog

use a Period .

Draw a
picture

The baby climbed out of the cot with the dot pattern and ate the hot pot.

cot
cama

dot
ponto

hot
quente

pot
panela

Name: _________________________ Date: _________________

Today is: [ Monday ] [ Tuesday ] [ Wednesday ]
[ Thursday ] [ Friday ]

Direction: Read the words and make a sentence.

| **fun** | **gun** | **run** | **sun** |
|---|---|---|---|
| diversão | arma de fogo | corre | sol |

Name _______________________

<table>
<tr><td>Draw a Picture</td><td>I Can...</td></tr>
</table>

**Draw a Picture**

**I Can...**

☐ use a Capital Letter
The cat is big.

☐ use spaces

☐ sound out words
d-o-g = dog

☐ use a Period .

☐ Draw a picture

Name: _____________________ Date: _____________

Today is: Monday  Tuesday  Wednesday  Thursday  Friday

Name: _________________ Date: _______________

Today is: Monday  Tuesday  Wednesday
Thursday  Friday

Direction: Read the words and make a sentence.

| bag | rag | tag | wag |
|-----|-----|-----|-----|
| saco | trapo | tag | abanando |

Name

Draw a Picture

## I Can...

- [ ] use a Capital Letter
  The cat is big.

- [ ] use spaces

- [ ] sound out words
  d-o-g = dog

- [ ] use a Period .

- [ ] Draw a picture

Name: _______________________  Date: _______________________

Today is: Monday  Tuesday  Wednesday  Thursday  Friday

Name: ___________________ Date: ___________________

Today is: | Monday | Tuesday | Wednesday |
| Thursday | Friday |

Direction: Read the words and make a sentence.

| **can** | **man** | **pan** | **van** |
|---|---|---|---|
| latas | cara | panela | furgão |

Name

Draw a Picture

## I Can...

- [ ] use a Capital Letter
  The cat is big.

- [ ] use spaces

- [ ] sound out words
  d-o-g = dog

- [ ] use a Period .

- [ ] Draw a picture

Name: _______________________ Date: _______________

Today is: Monday  Tuesday  Wednesday

Thursday  Friday

Name: _______________________  Date: _______________

Today is: Monday  Tuesday  Wednesday  Thursday  Friday

Direction: Read the words and make a sentence.

| **cut** | **gut** | **hut** | **nut** |
|---|---|---|---|
| cortar | intestino | cabana | noz |

Name

Draw a Picture

## I Can...

- [ ] use a Capital Letter
  The cat is big.

- [ ] use spaces

- [ ] sound out words
  d-o-g = dog

- [ ] use a Period  .

- [ ] Draw a picture

Name: _______________ Date: _______________

Today is: Monday Tuesday Wednesday Thursday Friday

Name: _______________  Date: _______________

Today is: Monday  Tuesday  Wednesday  Thursday  Friday

Direction: Read the words and make a sentence.

| **fat** | **cat** | **hat** | **mat** |
|---|---|---|---|
| gordura | gato | chapéu | esteira |

Name ___________________________

<table>
<tr><td>

Draw a Picture

</td><td>

## I Can...

☐ use a Capital Letter
<u>T</u>he cat is big.

☐ use spaces

☐ sound out words
d-o-g = dog

☐ use a Period .

☐ Draw a
picture

</td></tr>
</table>

Name: _______________________ Date: _______________

Today is: Monday  Tuesday  Wednesday
Thursday  Friday

Name: _________________________ Date: _________________________

Today is: Monday  Tuesday  Wednesday

Thursday  Friday

Direction: Read the words and make a sentence.

| cab | lab | tab | crab |
|---|---|---|---|
| táxi | laboratório | aba | caranguejo |

Name

Draw a Picture

## I Can...

- [ ] use a Capital Letter
  The cat is big.

- [ ] use spaces

- [ ] sound out words
  d-o-g = dog

- [ ] use a Period .

- [ ] Draw a picture

Name: _______________________  Date: _______________________

Today is:  Monday  Tuesday  Wednesday

Thursday  Friday

Name: _______________________ Date: _______________

Today is:  [ Monday ]  [ Tuesday ]  [ Wednesday ]
           [ Thursday ]  [ Friday ]

Direction: Read the words and make a sentence.

| ham | jam | ram | clam |
| --- | --- | --- | --- |
| presunto | geléia | ovelha | concha |

Name ____________________

Draw a Picture

## I Can...

☐ use a Capital Letter
The cat is big.

☐ use spaces

☐ sound out words
d-o-g = dog

☐ use a Period .

☐ Draw a picture

Name: _______________________     Date: _______________

Today is: Monday  Tuesday  Wednesday  Thursday  Friday

Name: ___________________  Date: ___________________

Today is: [ Monday ] [ Tuesday ] [ Wednesday ]
[ Thursday ] [ Friday ]

Direction: Read the words and make a sentence.

| **bed** | **led** | **red** | **wed** |
| --- | --- | --- | --- |
| cama | conduzindo | vermelho | casamento |

Name

Draw a Picture

## I Can...

- [ ] use a Capital Letter
  The cat is big.

- [ ] use spaces

- [ ] sound out words
  d-o-g = dog

- [ ] use a Period .

- [ ] Draw a picture

Name: _______________________  Date: _______________________

Today is: Monday  Tuesday  Wednesday
          Thursday  Friday

Name: _______________  Date: _______________

Today is: Monday  Tuesday  Wednesday  Thursday  Friday

Direction: Read the words and make a sentence.

| **bad** | **dad** | **mad** | **sad** |
|---|---|---|---|
| ruim | papai | louco | triste |

Name ______________________________

<table>
<tr><td>

Draw a Picture

</td><td>

## I Can...

☐ use a Capital Letter
<u>T</u>he cat is big.

☐ use spaces

☐ sound out words
d-o-g = dog

☐ use a Period  .

☐ Draw a
picture

</td></tr>
</table>

Name: _______________________  Date: _______________________

Today is:  Monday   Tuesday   Wednesday   Thursday   Friday

Name: _________________ Date: _________________

Today is: Monday   Tuesday   Wednesday

Thursday   Friday

Direction: Read the words and make a sentence.

| den | hen | pen | ten |
|-----|-----|-----|-----|
| covil | galinha | estábulos | dez |

Name

Draw a Picture

## I Can...

- [ ] use a Capital Letter
  The cat is big.

- [ ] use spaces

- [ ] sound out words
  d-o-g = dog

- [ ] use a Period .

- [ ] Draw a picture

Name: _______________________  Date: _______________________

Today is: Monday | Tuesday | Wednesday | Thursday | Friday

Name: ________________  Date: ________________

Today is: [Monday] [Tuesday] [Wednesday]
[Thursday] [Friday]

Direction: Read the words and make a sentence.

| **gum** | **mum** | **sum** | **drum** |
|---|---|---|---|
| gomoso | mãe | soma | tambor |

Name

Draw a Picture

## I Can...

- [ ] use a Capital Letter
  The cat is big.

- [ ] use spaces

- [ ] sound out words
  d-o-g = dog

- [ ] use a Period .

- [ ] Draw a picture

Name: ______________________  Date: ______________________

Today is: [ Monday ] [ Tuesday ] [ Wednesday ]
[ Thursday ] [ Friday ]

| bid | hid | kid | lid |
|-----|-----|-----|-----|
| licitação | ocultar | criança | tampa |

Name

Draw a Picture

## I Can...

- [ ] use a Capital Letter
  The cat is big.

- [ ] use spaces

- [ ] sound out words
  d-o-g = dog

- [ ] use a Period .

- [ ] Draw a picture

Name: ___________________  Date: ___________________

Today is: Monday  Tuesday  Wednesday  Thursday  Friday

Name: _________________  Date: _________________

Today is: | Monday | Tuesday | Wednesday |
| Thursday | Friday |

Direction: Read the words and make a sentence.

| **big** | **dig** | **pig** | **wig** |
| grande | escavação | porco | peruca |

Name

Draw a Picture

## I Can...

- [ ] use a Capital Letter
  The cat is big.

- [ ] use spaces

- [ ] sound out words
  d-o-g = dog

- [ ] use a Period .

- [ ] Draw a picture

Name: __________________ Date: __________________

Today is: Monday  Tuesday  Wednesday
          Thursday  Friday

Name: _______________ Date: _______________

Today is: | Monday | Tuesday | Wednesday |
| Thursday | Friday |

Direction: Read the words and make a sentence.

| **bin** | **fin** | **pin** | **win** |
|---|---|---|---|
| bin | barbatana | pin | ganhar |

Name

Draw a Picture

## I Can...

- [ ] use a Capital Letter
  The cat is big.

- [ ] use spaces

- [ ] sound out words
  d-o-g = dog

- [ ] use a Period .

- [ ] Draw a picture

Name: _________________________ Date: _______________

Today is:  [Monday]  [Tuesday]  [Wednesday]
           [Thursday]  [Friday]

Name: _______________________  Date: _______________________

Today is:  Monday   Tuesday   Wednesday

Thursday   Friday

Direction: Read the words and make a sentence.

| **hip** | **lip** | **nip** | **sip** |
|---|---|---|---|
| quadril | lábios | beliscar | bebida |

Name

Draw a Picture

## I Can...

- [ ] use a Capital Letter
The cat is big.

- [ ] use spaces

- [ ] sound out words
d-o-g = dog

- [ ] use a Period  .

- [ ] Draw a picture

Name: _______________________ Date: _______________

Today is: Monday Tuesday Wednesday Thursday Friday

Name: _______________________  Date: _______________________

Today is: Monday | Tuesday | Wednesday | Thursday | Friday

Direction: Read the words and make a sentence.

| fit | hit | kit | sit |
|-----|-----|-----|-----|
| em forma | acertar | kit | sentar |

Name _______________________

<table>
<tr><td>

**Draw a Picture**

</td><td>

## I Can...

☐ use a Capital Letter
The cat is big.

☐ use spaces

☐ sound out words
d-o-g = dog

☐ use a Period .

☐ Draw a picture

</td></tr>
</table>

Name: _______________________  Date: _______________

Today is: [ Monday ] [ Tuesday ] [ Wednesday ]
          [ Thursday ] [ Friday ]

Name: __________________ Date: __________________

Today is: Monday    Tuesday    Wednesday    Thursday    Friday

Direction: Read the words and make a sentence.

| cob | job | rob | sob |
|-----|-----|-----|-----|
| milho | trabalho | roubar | chorar |

Name

Draw a Picture

## I Can...

- [ ] use a Capital Letter
  The cat is big.

- [ ] use spaces

- [ ] sound out words
  d-o-g = dog

- [ ] use a Period .

- [ ] Draw a picture

Name: _______________________ Date: _______________

Today is: Monday  Tuesday  Wednesday  Thursday  Friday

Name: _________________________ Date: _________________

Today is: Monday | Tuesday | Wednesday
Thursday | Friday

Direction: Read the words and make a sentence.

| **dog** | **hog** | **jog** | **log** |
|---|---|---|---|
| cão | porco | corrida | madeira |

Name

Draw a Picture

## I Can...

- [ ] use a Capital Letter
  The cat is big.

- [ ] use spaces

- [ ] sound out words
  d-o-g = dog

- [ ] use a Period .

- [ ] Draw a picture

Name: _______________________  Date: _______________________

Today is: Monday  Tuesday  Wednesday  Thursday  Friday

Name: _______________________  Date: _______________________

Today is:  [ Monday ]  [ Tuesday ]  [ Wednesday ]

[ Thursday ]  [ Friday ]

Direction: Read the words and make a sentence.

| **bug** | **hug** | **jug** | **mug** |
|---|---|---|---|
| erro | abraço | jarro | caneca |

Name

Draw a Picture

## I Can...

- [ ] use a Capital Letter
  The cat is big.

- [ ] use spaces

- [ ] sound out words
  d-o-g = dog

- [ ] use a Period .

- [ ] Draw a picture

Name: _____________________ Date: _____________

Today is: Monday | Tuesday | Wednesday
Thursday | Friday

Name: _______________________  Date: _______________________

Today is: [ Monday ] [ Tuesday ] [ Wednesday ]
[ Thursday ] [ Friday ]

Direction: Read the words and make a sentence.

| cot | dot | hot | pot |
|-----|-----|-----|-----|
| cama | ponto | quente | panela |

Name

Draw a Picture

## I Can...

- [ ] use a Capital Letter
  The cat is big.

- [ ] use spaces

- [ ] sound out words
  d-o-g = dog

- [ ] use a Period .

- [ ] Draw a picture

Name: _______________________    Date: _______________

Today is: | Monday | Tuesday | Wednesday |
| Thursday | Friday |